FORENSIC SCIENCE

Crime and Detection series

- Criminal Terminology
- Cyber Crime
- Daily Prison Life
- Death Row and Capital Punishment
- Domestic Crime
- Famous Prisons
- Famous Trials
- Forensic Science
- Government Intelligence Agencies
- Hate Crimes
- The History and Methods of Torture
- The History of Punishment
- International Terrorism
- Major Unsolved Crimes
- Organized Crime
- Protecting Yourself Against Criminals
- Race and Crime
- Serial Murders
- The United States Justice System
- The War Against Drugs

CRIME AND DETECTION

FORENSIC SCIENCE

BRIAN INNES

MASON CREST PUBLISHERS
www.masoncrest.com

Mason Crest Publishers Inc.
370 Reed Road
Broomall, PA 19008
(866) MCP-BOOK (toll free)
www.masoncrest.com

2 3 4 5 6 7 8 9 10

Innes, Brian.
   Forensic science / Brian Innes.
      v. cm. -- (Crime and detection)
Includes bibliographical references and index.
Contents: Every contact leaves a trace -- Finger of fate -- Deadly poison -- Telltale blood -- The smoking gun -- Fragments of evidence.

   ISBN 1-59084-373-8

   1. Forensic sciences--Juvenile literature. 2. Crime laboratories--Juvenile literature. 3. Criminal investigation--Juvenile literature. 4. Criminals--Identification--Juvenile literature. 5. Evidence, Criminal--Juvenile literature. [1. Forensic sciences. 2. Crime laboratories. 3. Criminal investigation. 4. Criminals--Identification.] I. Title. II. Series.

   HV8073.I445 2003
   363.25--dc21

                                                    2003000479

Editorial and design by
Amber Books Ltd.
Bradley's Close
74–77 White Lion Street
London N1 9PF
www.amberbooks.co.uk

Project Editor: Michael Spilling
Design: Floyd Sayers
Picture Research: Natasha Jones

Printed and bound in Malaysia

Picture credits
Corbis: 85; Mary Evans Picture Library: 23, 24, 36, 39, 52; PA Photos: 40; Pictor International: 14; Popperfoto: 6, 8, 10, 11, 13, 17, 18, 20, 26, 30, 32, 43, 44, 47, 49, 54, 57, 58, 61, 64, 66, 69, 70, 75, 76, 79, 82, 83, 84, 86, 88, 89; The Wellcome Trust Medical Photographic Library: 34, 62, 74; Topham Picturepoint: 50, 59, 73, 87; U.S. National Archives: 29
Front cover: The Wellcome Trust Medical Photographic Library (background), Popperfoto

CONTENTS

Introduction

From the moment in the Book of Genesis when Cain's envy of his brother Abel erupted into violence, crime has been an inescapable feature of human life. Every society ever known has had its own sense of how things ought to be, its deeply held views on how men and women should behave. Yet in every age there have been individuals ready to break these rules for their own advantage: they must be resisted if the community is to thrive.

This exciting and vividly illustrated series of books sets out the history of crime and detection from the earliest times to the present day, from the empires of the ancient world to the towns and cities of the 21st century. From the commandments of the great religions to the theories of modern psychologists, it considers changing attitudes toward offenders and their actions. Contemporary crime is examined in its many different forms: everything from racial hatred to industrial espionage, from serial murder to drug trafficking, from international terrorism to domestic violence.

The series looks, too, at the heroic work of those men and women entrusted with the task of overseeing and maintaining law and order, from judges and court officials to police officers and other law enforcement agents. The tools and techniques at their disposal are described in detail, and the ethical issues they face are concisely and clearly explained.

All in all, the *Crime and Detection* series provides a comprehensive and accessible account of this exciting world, in theory and in practice, past and present.

CHARLIE FULLER

Executive Director, International Association of Undercover Officers

Left: The search for evidence—FBI investigators comb the debris scattered from the crash of United Airlines Flight 93 near Shanksville, PA. This was one of the four planes that were hijacked on September 11, 2001, but was forced to the ground by the heroic self-sacrifice of the passengers.

Every Contact Leaves a Trace

Crime can take many different forms—from petty theft and forgery to violent murder—and science can be used to help solve nearly every case. The word "forensic" means "connected with the courtroom"; so forensic science is, therefore, concerned with gathering hard evidence that can be presented at trial.

The most important cases in which detailed scientific evidence is required are those involving brutal assault, rape, and death. This is why, in the early days of forensic science, most of those who gave evidence were medical practitioners and the practice was long known as "medical jurisprudence." Gradually, however, different areas of specialization have been developed, and now, as well as medical examiners, there are experts in **ballistics**, **toxicology**, **serology**, and many other disciplines.

Early in the 20th century, a French scientist, Dr. Edmond Locard, laid down the basic principle for investigating the scene of a crime: "Every contact leaves a trace." That is, every criminal leaves something behind at the scene: a weapon; a spent bullet; a print from a finger, hand, or even ear; the track of a shoe; a hair; or a minute fragment of something. And he (or she) also carries something away: powder residue from a gun, a tiny splash of blood, a scratch made by the victim, dust or dirt, or a single fiber from the

Left: A British "SOCO" (scene-of-crime officer), properly dressed in white coveralls and overshoes, which can later be examined forensically for additional trace evidence. He is carrying an evidence bag from a plane, hijacked by Afghan refugees, which landed at Stansted Airport, London, England, on February 10, 2000.

It is absolutely essential that the scene of a crime be sealed off as soon as possible to avoid contaminating the site with unconnected contact traces. Ideally, access should be restricted to the medical examiner and the forensic officer and his or her search team.

victim's clothing. It is the job of the forensic scientist to detect, examine, and analyze these traces to secure evidence for a susequent trial.

"EYES OPEN, MOUTH SHUT, HANDS IN POCKETS"

When a crime scene is discovered, it is essential that it be contained and sealed off quickly to preserve any trace evidence. This is often difficult. In the case of a suspicious death, for example, the scene will be disturbed by the person who found the body, the first uniformed officers to arrive, the ambulance crew, and the medical examiner or coroner who pronounces the body dead.

The crime scene investigator will arrive as soon as possible, and will allow as few people as are necessary within the closed-off area. If the scene is out in the open, however, there are already likely to be many footprints, for example, that are not connected with the crime. Indoors, the body may have been moved and the clothing loosened in attempts at artificial respiration. In addition, significant items in the room may also have been moved in some way.

The investigating officer must always remember the rule "Eyes open, mouth shut, and hands in pockets." He (it is still more often than not a man, though this is changing) must use his eyes to take in every detail of

Every piece of trace evidence should be identified, marked on a grid plan of the crime scene, and photographed. Each is then placed individually in a plastic bag or box and labeled with full details. When items of evidence pass from the custody of one person to another, they should be logged and signed for.

the scene. He must avoid saying anything that could affect the testimony of someone nearby who may later have to give evidence. And he should touch nothing until the rest of his search team arrives.

KEEPING THE EVIDENCE RELIABLE

The task of searching a death scene is to find anything that should not be there. First of all, photographs or video recordings are taken, not only of the body, but also of any visible traces. This includes all footprints, tire tracks, marks on tree trunks, signs of a struggle, bloodstains, or any objects possibly used for assault. Ideally, the investigator should make a tape recording of everything that is done and of everything he sees.

Then the detailed search begins. Every physical object must be collected, either with latex-gloved fingers or forceps, and placed in a plastic bag or box. This must be labeled with full details of where and when it was found. Its position can also be marked on a grid plan of the area. Every time such an item of evidence passes from the custody of one person to another, it should be signed for and logged. This is called the "chain of custody." Any gap in this chain may be seized on by defense counsel at trial as an indication that the forensic evidence is not to be relied upon.

The search must be carried out as soon as possible, particularly if the crime scene is outdoors. Fingerprints can be searched for later, since they generally survive for a long time. Similarly, bloodstains are scraped up for later analysis, and materials such as dust and fibers are collected with a miniature vacuum cleaner.

IN THE AUTOPSY ROOM

The word "autopsy" means "seeing for oneself." This is what the medical examiner or **pathologist** does, examining the dead body in detail. In the case of rape, however, the surviving victim is examined.

First of all, it must be confirmed that a body is dead. There have been many occasions when a "corpse" has revived in the mortuary or even at the

CHAIN OF CUSTODY

It was a combination of doubts about the chain of custody of forensic evidence that contributed to the acquittal of O.J. Simpson (pictured below) in his criminal trial for the murders of his wife Nicole and waiter Ronald Goldman in California in 1994. Apparently firm evidence included blood splashes found at the scene said to match Simpson's blood type, a pair of socks soaked with the victims' blood found at the foot of his bed, and a similarly bloodstained glove.

It emerged in court that a vial sample of blood taken from Simpson had decreased in volume while in police custody. Two experts for the defense, who had examined the socks two weeks after the murder, testified that they found no bloodstains. Furthermore, the prosecution admitted that the stains were not reported until four weeks later. Samples taken from the socks

were analyzed by the FBI and were found to contain a preservative. The glove was said to be too tight for Simpson's hand and, when the officer who claimed to have found the glove admitted perjuring himself with earlier evidence, the case fell apart.

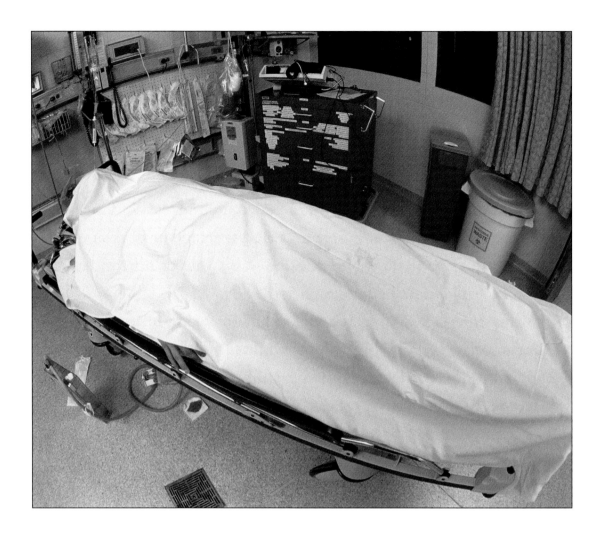

The modern autopsy room is strikingly different from the old-fashioned morgue. It is efficiently organized, with every necessary piece of equipment in its place. Here, the sheeted body of a dead person lies on a stainless steel gurney, awaiting transfer to the dissection table for post mortem examination.

beginning of an autopsy. In rural districts, the first pronouncement may have been made by the coroner, an elected individual who is quite possibly only the local **mortician**. (It may be a popular myth, but it is said of one rural coroner, summoned to a gunshot death, that he announced: "Death by natural causes—in this county, death by gunshot is natural.")

The autopsy is devoted to determining the cause of death. If the body belongs to an unknown person, the **postmortem** examination may provide clues to help in identification. Equally important is an estimation of the time of death. Until recently, it was customary for the first medically qualified person at the scene to take the body's temperature, but this could interfere with the pathologist's subsequent examination for trace evidence. For this reason, it is preferable to leave this estimation to the autopsy.

ESTIMATING THE TIME OF DEATH

The human body begins to lose internal heat from the moment of death. A clothed body of average build shows a fall in temperature of around 3.2°F per hour for the first six to eight hours. After that time has elapsed, the body cools less rapidly. However, unclothed bodies cool more rapidly, and fat bodies more slowly. The rate of cooling is also related to the temperature of the surroundings. In very hot climates, for example, the body may even become warmer after death. It is therefore difficult to place an estimation of time of death within greater accuracy than three to four hours.

Another possible indication is the phenomenon known as **rigor mortis**. The muscles of the face begin to stiffen within one to four hours and the limbs in four to six hours. After 12 hours, in normal conditions, the body is rigid, and then gradually relaxes as decomposition of the tissues begins. However, these changes are also widely variable. It has been claimed that analysis of the various body fluids can provide a more accurate estimation of time of death, but there is no way of knowing how physical or emotional conditions can have affected their chemical nature.

Throughout the examination of the body, the pathologist records every stage on tape; a video may also be made of the entire operation, or photographs taken of significant details that are revealed. First, the outward appearance of the corpse must be described: racial type, physical features, and clothing, which may show signs of weapon attack. Fingerprints may be taken, and casts taken of the shoes, to eliminate some of the footprints taken at the crime scene. Then the clothing is carefully removed and bagged, and the examiner records in precise detail the external appearance of the body.

EXTERNAL PHYSICAL CLUES

The color of the body is important, since it may indicate poisoning, particularly by carbon monoxide from incompletely combusted house gas or car exhaust fumes. All bruises and wounds must be recorded in detail. The condition of the eyes can reveal if the person has died of **asphyxiation** or drug poisoning. Any marks of injections are also recorded since they can provide important clues. The body must also be examined for **hypostasis**.

Hypostasis, also known as postmortem lividity, sets in at the moment of death. When you die, your heart stops beating, your blood ceases to circulate, and gravity causes your blood to settle gradually to the lowest parts of your body. The red **corpuscles** are the first to settle, forming pinkish-blue patches after one to three hours. In six to eight hours, these patches have joined up into larger purplish-red areas.

Where the weight of the body presses against a hard surface, they do not form. So in a body lying on its back, hypostasis appears on the back of the neck, the small of the back, and the thighs. In a number of cases, the presence of hypostasis in the "wrong" areas is evidence that a body has been moved some time after death.

THE INTERNAL EXAMINATION

Now the internal examination of the body begins. First, swab specimens are taken from sites such as the hands, mouth, breasts, vagina, and rectum. In cases of sexual assault, the pubic hair is combed in the hope of discovering hairs that do not belong to the victim. Then the pathologist takes up a large, sharp knife and makes a Y-shaped cut that begins behind each ear and extends down the body as far as the groin. This makes it possible to peel back the skin and expose the bones and muscles of the neck and chest, as well as the internal organs, and perhaps reveal bruising that did not show up externally. If necessary, the pathologist can make similar incisions to the victim's back.

All wounds are explored and described, particularly the tracks made by

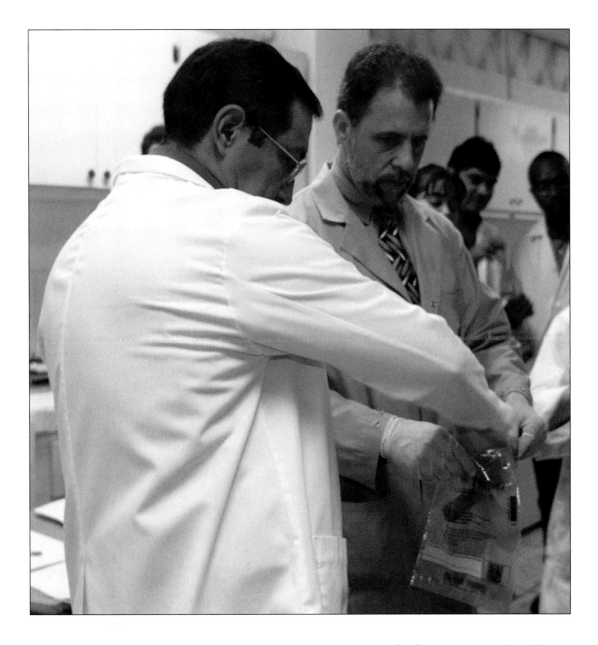

When the remains of four persons were found during excavation of a former Panamanian military base in January 2001, it was important to identify them. Dr Vicente Pachal—assisted by Dr. Daniel Demers from the Genetics and IVF Institute of Virginia—bagged the evidence for further anthropological examination.

any bullets. Tissue samples are taken from every injury. In addition, broken bones and damaged cartilage must be detected, particularly those of the neck, if strangulation is suspected.

Next, the lungs, heart, liver, kidneys, stomach, and other organs, must be removed for further examination and analysis. To reach them, the breast-bone has to be cut through. After this, the skull must be opened. The first incision is continued across the top of the head so that the skin can be pulled away from the bone. A power saw is used to cut around the skull so that the top can be pulled off. The pathologist examines the inside of the skull and the brain for signs of injury, and then the brain is removed for later examination. An experienced examiner can sometimes complete all these operations within 30 minutes.

Whenever possible, forensic investigators should wear white coveralls, overshoes, and latex gloves. When TV presenter Francisco Stanley was killed in a hail of bullets in central Mexico City, a police scientist took the body of the victim, and the shattered windscreen of his car, for detailed examination.

ODOR AS EVIDENCE

Sometimes, while carrying out the autopsy, the examiner will detect signs that suggest poisoning. Substances such as ammonia, carbolic acid, and cyanide have characteristic odors. (There is a story that one eminent English pathologist could smell cyanide only if he was smoking!) One unusual case concerned a young girl who was found dead in bed. When her skull was opened, her brain smelled unmistakably of the cleaning fluid carbon tetrachloride, which she had been in the habit of sniffing, and which had eventually killed her.

FURTHER DETAILED EXAMINATION

If the victim has been in a fire or was apparently drowned, the examiner will search the air passages for traces of soot or water. These can only have been inhaled before death. The condition of the liver and kidneys is also reported at the autopsy. The liver may show signs of **cirrhosis** or **hepatitis** although many drugs, particularly an overdose of the painkiller paracetamol, can produce similar symptoms. Inflammation of the kidneys can indicate the presence of poisonous mercury compounds, lead poisoning, or long-term abuse of phenacetin, a compound used to ease pain or fever.

The pathologist's work in the autopsy room is now finished. All the tissue samples and organs must be further examined and analyzed by specialists. Casts of the jaws are taken by an odontologist, an expert who can then compare the casts with dental records to confirm the identity. If identification is necessary, a forensic anthropologist will examine the body (particularly the bones). Everything is preserved in the mortuary until the inquest is over. Any samples that provide critical evidence will be stored, even in some instances for a long time after the case is declared officially closed.

Finger of Fate

In 1877, Englishman William Herschel was appointed to be a magistrate in India. One of his duties was to pay government pensions, but he was suspicious that relatives were impersonating pensioners who had died. So he made every pensioner sign a receipt with the prints of two fingers of the right hand. He observed that the prints did not change with age and seemed to be unique to each individual. He speculated they might be valuable in the keeping of criminal records.

At the same time, a Scottish physician named Henry Faulds was working in a hospital in Tokyo, Japan. He noted that many illiterate people "signed" documents with a handprint, and he began to collect specimen prints to compare. In 1879, a thief climbed over the garden wall of a house in Tokyo, leaving a sooty handprint. When he heard that the police had already arrested a suspect, Dr. Faulds asked permission to compare the prints, and showed that the suspect was not the thief. Soon after, another man confessed to the crime, and Faulds demonstrated that his handprint matched that on the wall.

Realizing that what he now called "**dactylography**" had criminological importance, Faulds wrote a letter to the leading English scientific journal *Nature* describing his findings. When William Herschel retired from the Indian Civil Service in the same year, he was deeply disappointed to discover that Faulds had preempted his discovery. He, too, wrote to *Nature*, provoking further letters from other readers for and against his suggestions. Nine years passed before the English physician and **anthropologist** Sir

Left: The standard method of dusting for fingerprints has not changed in 100 years. In a search for terrorist suspects, following the destruction of the World Trade Center on September 11, 2001, an FBI crime scene investigator inspects a door at the home of one such suspect in Florida.

Francis Galton remembered the correspondence in *Nature,* and began to think of a way of classifying fingerprints.

CLASSIFYING FINGERPRINTS

The principal problem lay in the wide variety of patterns on the fingertips, which would make the comparison of prints a long and difficult procedure. At last, after studying hundreds of prints that he had collected, Galton noticed that nearly every one included a small triangular area where the lines came together. He called this a "delta"—from the Greek letter D—and divided his prints into four types: those with no delta, those with a delta leaning to the left, those with a delta leaning to the right, and those with several deltas. If all 10 fingerprints of a person were available, they could be classified into more than 60,000 individual types. In 1892, Galton detailed his findings in his book, *Fingerprints.*

The book was newly published when a policeman in Argentina named Juan Vucetich decided to put Galton's discovery to practical use. In June of that year, he successfully applied it in the case of a mother who had murdered her two children. By 1894, the Argentine police force had become the first in the world to adopt fingerprints as a means of criminal identification, and the technique soon spread throughout South America.

The development of fingerprinting took a slightly different direction in Europe and the United States, however, becoming based upon a more detailed method of classification proposed by Edward Henry. Henry was Inspector General of the Bengal Police in India when he read Galton's book and decided to pursue his own research. In addition to the deltas, he found five more-clearly defined types of patterns in the fingertip lines: arches; "tented" arches; radial loops (that is, loops leaning toward the radius bone on the outside of the arm); ulnar loops, leaning toward the inner ulnar bone; and whorls.

Henry's system was adopted by the Bengal government in 1897, and their office in Calcutta became the first national fingerprint bureau in the

English scientist Sir Francis Galton was involved in the investigation of heredity and intelligence. Unimpressed by the work of French criminologist Alphonse Bertillon in the identification of criminals by their physical measurements, Galton published the first detailed study of fingerprints in 1892.

HENRY'S FIRST SUCCESS

Edward Henry had among his assistants a Detective Sergeant Charles Collins, who began to take photographs of fingerprints. In June 1902, a thief broke into a house in south London and left some dirty hand marks on a windowsill. Collins photographed a thumbprint and then set about comparing it with those of previously convicted criminals. After a painstaking search, he was able to identify the print as that of Henry Jackson, who was arrested just a few days later.

In court, Collins demonstrated to the jury how fingerprints were identified and produced his photographs. The jury was convinced, Jackson was found guilty, and the principle of fingerprint identification entered British law.

world. In 1901, Henry was appointed Assistant Commissioner of London's Metropolitan Police and given the task of establishing a Fingerprint Branch at Scotland Yard.

One of the officers of the Fingerprint Branch was sent in 1904 to the St. Louis World's Fair and Exposition, and while there he gave a number of lectures on the Henry system. The Department of Justice had already made the decision to allocate a sum "not to exceed $60" for a fingerprinting exercise at Leavenworth Prison in Texas. In 1905, the technique was adopted at Sing Sing and other prisons in New York State and by the St. Louis police the following year. The U.S. Army, Navy, and Marine Corps, too, began to fingerprint both enlisted men and officers.

Soon, however, some way of coordinating these separate records had to be found, and the Department of Justice undertook the necessary arrangements. Unfortunately, they gave the cataloging task to Leavenworth, where it was soon discovered that the convicts doing the work were taking the opportunity to falsify the records to their own advantage. The International Association of Chiefs of Police (IACP) campaigned for the proper centralization of fingerprint records, and what was later to become the FBI was set up within the Department of Justice in Washington, D.C. It was not until 1924, however, when J. Edgar Hoover was made Director of the Bureau, that he found himself faced with the job of cataloging some 800,000 records, haphazardly piled in storage.

DETECTING FINGERPRINTS

At first, police investigators were concerned only with visible prints—those that were dirty, bloody, or impressed into a soft surface. Quite soon, however, researchers discovered that invisible, or **latent**, prints could be detected on most smooth surfaces. These latent prints are formed by traces of sweat, and in many cases can be almost permanent—they have even been found on objects in ancient tombs.

Such prints must be "developed" to make them visible. The basic technique that is still employed is to dust an area with a very fine powder, using either a fine camelhair brush or an "insufflator," which is not unlike a scent sprayer. A device known as a Magna-Brush™ uses magnetic powder. Colored and fluorescent powders are also available. In earlier days, these developed prints then had to be photographed, but now, most prints are "lifted" with transparent adhesive tape, which can then be mounted on thin cardboard or a transparent backing.

Prints on porous surfaces, such as thin cardboard or wood, are developed in other ways. For some 50 years, development was achieved using silver nitrate, which reacts with the salt in sweat. Otherwise, iodine vapor, which

Forensics experts inspect a car and dust for fingerprints after the shooting of a high-ranking official in Mexico City. It is vital for investigators to treat every piece of material evidence as a possible lead that will implicate the criminals.

ACCEPTED AS EVIDENCE IN THE U.S.

The first criminal case in which fingerprints were established as acceptable evidence in the United States was that of *The People v. Jennings,* decided on appeal in the Illinois Supreme Court, December 21, 1911.

Thomas Jennings had broken into a home in Chicago, leaving prints on a newly painted porch railing as he did so, and had shot the owner. Shortly afterward, he was detained for being in possession of a loaded gun, but the arresting officers at that time had no knowledge of the murder. It was only when his fingerprints were compared with those on the railing that his guilt became apparent.

reacts with the grease, could be used. Then, in the 1950s, it was found that a substance called ninhydrin would react with the amino acids in sweat, producing a purplish image. Other techniques make use of dyes that react with proteins in sweat.

Fingerprints on human skin, which can be especially valuable as evidence in cases of rape, seldom survive for more than an hour or two. However, if they are quickly searched for, they can be lifted on high-gloss Kromecote paper or illuminated by specialized x-ray methods.

The search for latent prints can take a long time. Every surface at the crime scene must be examined. In recent years, however, it has been found that prints exposed to the fumes of "super glue" will show up white on dark surfaces. This is particularly useful in the examination of enclosed spaces, such as car interiors and cupboards, where the fumes can be concentrated. Another important discovery has been that laser beams will reveal prints— even old ones—and therefore do not affect the object on which they are found.

LASERS UNMASK A WAR CRIMINAL

In 1975, the Department of Justice sought a deportation order against Valerian Trifa, a former archbishop of the Romanian Orthodox Church who had concealed his former membership of the Iron Guard, Romania's pro-Nazi party.

It was not until 1982, however, that the West German government discovered a compromising postcard in their archives that Trifa had written to a high-ranking Nazi official. They refused permission for the FBI to use any destructive technique on this historical document, but a laser revealed Trifa's thumbprint on the card, and he was deported in 1984.

ANALYZING PRINTS

When a person's fingerprints are recorded, two sets are taken. The first set is "rolled" prints. Each finger and the thumb is inked in turn and rolled onto a card so that the patterns extending around the edges of the finger are recorded. Then the same 10 prints are taken "plain." This is to ensure that both sets are made in the same sequence. There have been cases in which suspected criminals have held out their fingers in the wrong order, or even had the same hand printed twice. If it is a matter of comparing these prints directly with those found at a crime scene, the task is relatively simple, but in many cases, the question of identification arises.

Computer databases now make it possible to scan millions of records in a few minutes, but for many years, police investigators had to conduct manual searches for matching prints. As the number of files increased, this became a daunting task. In 1927, Scotland Yard's Detective Chief Inspector Harry Battley began to introduce a new cataloging system, more comprehensive than Henry's.

Battley designed a special magnifying glass with a glass base engraved with seven concentric circles, designated A to G. By centering the glass over the print, the circle in which it appeared could classify the position of the delta, or the absence of a delta noted. A separate collection of prints, classified for each finger, was made, and each of the 10 collections was subdivided into nine print types: Henry's five, and a further four types of loops. Known as the Single Print System, this is now the basis of all fingerprint

Taking a rolled fingerprint on a record card. A print of each finger and thumb is taken, and a similar set of 10 prints that are not rolled. Although this remains regular practice, modern computer systems can scan fingers and hands much quicker, and store the analyzed patterns on a database.

Security systems that identify people by scanning the pattern of lines on their fingertips have been installed in many government, commercial, and residential locations. Now a South Korean company has developed a compact computer device that scans the user's finger to establish identity in place of a password for Internet communications.

analysis throughout the world.

Today, it is not uncommon for new prints to be taken from a person by the use of an electronic scanner, which produces a standard fingerprint card. It is then possible to link the scanner directly to a database. Security systems using a similar principle have been installed in many government, commercial, and residential buildings. Problems arose, however, when it was found that different police authorities had purchased incompatible types of computers or software, making it impossible for one database to communicate with another, but national and even international databases are now being established worldwide.

OTHER TYPES OF PRINTS

After DCI Battley had established the Single Fingerprint System at Scotland Yard, he turned his attention to palm prints and showed that these were just as distinctive as fingerprints. He had his first success in 1931 in a case of burglary, but, as the suspect pleaded guilty on being shown the evidence, the case did not enter English law. It was not until 1942 that a palm print in a murder case was found to be acceptable evidence. In more recent

TRYING TO BEAT THE SYSTEM

Criminals make many attempts to avoid leaving fingerprints, for example, by wearing surgical gloves. In several cases, they have then carelessly discarded the gloves close to the crime scene, leaving clearly identifiable prints inside. Others have had their fingerprints scarred with acid or surgically altered, but often the print of the second joint has proved sufficient to identify them.

In 1990, a drug suspect was arrested in Miami whose fingertips were heavily scarred. He had sliced off the skin, cut it into small pieces, and transplanted them, creating a human jigsaw puzzle. An expert from the FBI spent weeks on the problem, working with enlarged photographs and matching the patterns of the lines. When he had fitted all the pieces together, they matched the prints of a man wanted in another drug case. So the FBI had found their man.

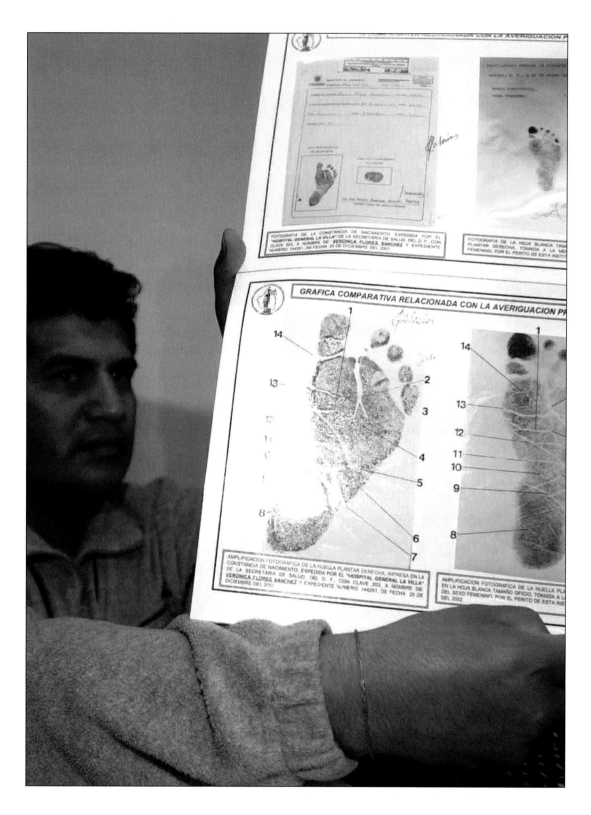

A proud father announces the return of his baby daughter following her abduction from a hospital in southern Mexico. Investigators were able positively to identify the baby from her finger- and footprints from the hospital birth records.

years, the print of an ear, left by a burglar as he listened against a window, has also been accepted.

A criminal may wear gloves, thinking that he or she will escape detection, but even that is not immune from science. Gerald Lambourne, who became head of the Scotland Yard's Fingerprint Department in 1973, began to study the prints left by gloves. His examination in hundreds of pairs of rubber gloves revealed that, even though thousands of gloves are manufactured, there are minute differences in the surface that make one pair of gloves distinct from another. He went on to study other types of glove, and had a success in 1971, when he showed that a pair with a suede finish in the possession of a burglary suspect matched a print on a broken window. Lambourne's findings have since been accepted by police forces in every part of the world.

Footprints can prove equally important as evidence. In 1945, a series of break-ins began in New York State. In the first two cases, the thief left fingerprints, but no matches could be found in police files. A year later, the print of an unusual overshoe was found, and in 1947, a sneaker print was discovered. An identical sneaker print was found some days later, together with fingerprints that matched those taken in 1945. Eventually, in November 1947, inquiries led to a suspect, who implicated his uncle. Searching the uncle's house, the police found both the overshoes and the sneakers, and his fingerprints matched those from the earlier burglaries. The two men eventually confessed to over 50 break-ins in the locality.

Finally, tire prints left at the crime scene can also provide a wealth of vital evidence. An expert can gain information about the age of a tire from the degree of wear, and can also extract information about the vehicle carrying it. Different makes of car are fitted with specific patterns of tires. In addition, the weight, and the way the vehicle is loaded, can be ascertained from the width of the print, while unevenness of the suspension will cause variations in wear. The incorrect alignment of the front wheels, causing "scrub," can also be detected.

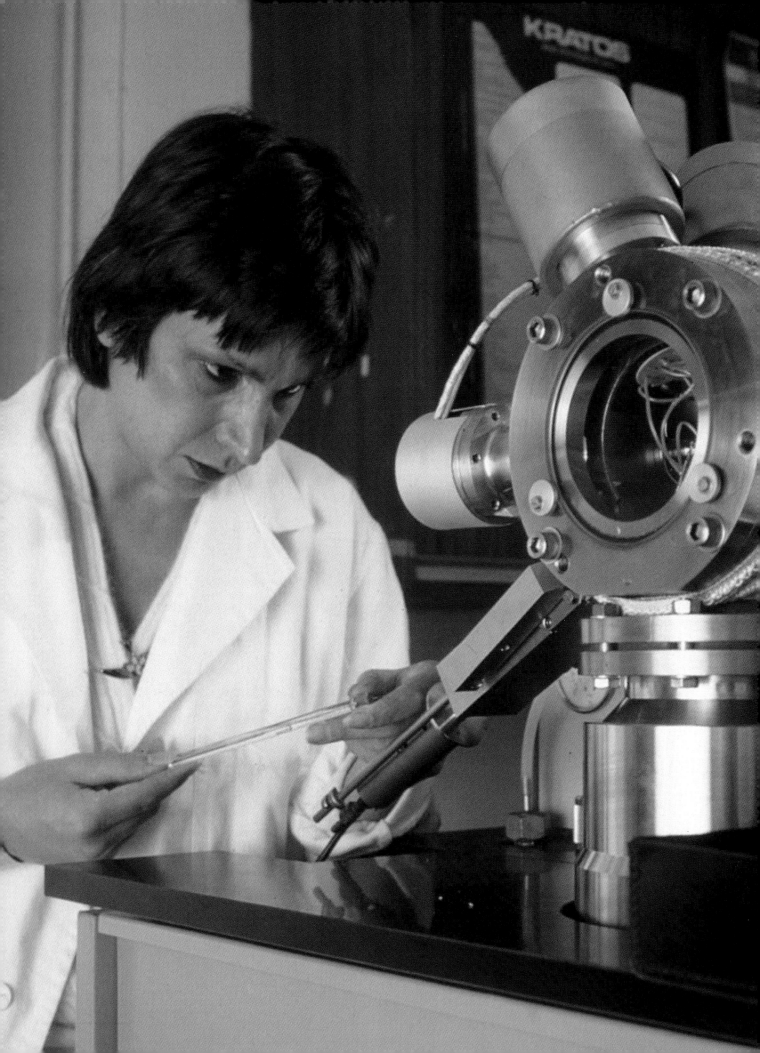

Deadly Poison

Most murders are carried out by brute force or with a weapon. But there is another method that is silent, secret, and insidious—poisoning. For many hundreds of years, there was no way of proving that someone had been killed by poison, because there was no way of identifying the poison in the dead body. For this reason, since as far back as the 17th century, poison has been known as "the coward's weapon."

Ancient peoples were aware of many poisons, which were mostly derived from vegetable sources. Today, their active principles, such as morphine, strychnine, nicotine, atropine, or ricin have been isolated, and all have been used as murderous poisons during the last two centuries. Mineral substances containing elements such as lead, antimony, mercury, thallium, phosphorus, or arsenic, are also highly toxic. Of these, arsenious oxide, commonly called arsenic became for a long time the poison of choice for murder. Because of its white color and sweetish taste, it could easily be disguised in the unsuspecting victim's food.

The science of chemistry was developed during the latter half of the 18th century. Since that time, and throughout the 19th century, scientists have found ways of preparing a wide range of pure toxic chemicals. However, for many years there was no sure means of detecting their presence after death. The study of poisons, known as toxicology, began with Mathieu Orfila. He was born in Minorca, one of the Spanish Balearic Islands, in 1787 and won a scholarship to Barcelona University. He then went on to study in Paris, France, gaining his medical degree. As he later

Left: Here, a laboratory technician uses a mass spectrometer to analyze the constituent parts of an organic compound. This technique has proved to be extremely effective in analysis when only minute quantities of substance are available.

wrote: "The central fact that struck me had never been perceived by anyone else... toxicology does not yet exist."

DEATH BY ARSENIC

Orfila published his first treatise on the subject in 1813 and soon became famous. In 1819, he was made Professor of Medical Jurisprudence in Paris and gave evidence in a number of poisoning cases. He turned his attention, in particular, to arsenic. He would not have met with success, however, had not an ingenious test for detecting tiny quantities of the element been developed during the 1830s by an English chemist named James Marsh. In 1839, using the Marsh test (which is still taught to students of chemistry), Orfila conclusively proved that Marie Lafarge, a Frenchwoman, had poisoned her husband.

Before the passing of legislation to control the sale of the poison, arsenic—white arsenious oxide—was readily available. Young English writer Thomas Chatterton was only 17 years old when, starving and penniless in London, he committed suicide by taking arsenic in 1770.

SCIENCE CATCHES UP WITH HISTORY

Modern analysis for tiny traces of arsenic and many other chemical elements can now be carried out by a process known as neutron activation. In 1968, it was used to solve a mystery nearly a century old.

American explorer Charles Hall died in November 1871 aboard his ship *Polaris* during a search for the North Pole. There were doubts, however, about his death. Many people believed that Emil Bessels, the doctor on the expedition, had poisoned him. In August 1968, two scientists flew to Hall's grave, some 500 miles from the North Pole, and exhumed the body, which had been preserved in the icy-cold ground. Neutron activation tests on a fingernail showed high arsenic content, and the analyst concluded, "Arsenic poisoning is a fair diagnosis."

Arsenic was widely used as a rat poison, and so, following the Lafarge case, most countries passed legislation restricting the sale of arsenic, requiring that its purchase be signed for and insisting that it be mixed with a colored substance. However, it continued to be employed in murder, although the perpetrators were usually discovered. As recently as 1935, arsenic was used by Mary Creighton and her lover Edward Appelgate to kill Appelgate's wife on Long Island, NY; and, even more recently, by Marie Hilley of Anniston, Alabama, who poisoned her husband with arsenic in 1975 and attempted to kill her daughter with it in 1979.

"MAD AS HATTERS"

Strictly speaking, the element arsenic is not regarded chemically as a metal, although it has similar properties. Other metallic elements, such as lead and mercury, can be equally toxic. In the 19th century, factories, such as those at Danbury, Connecticut, used mercuric salts to cure the felt for hats. Many people working on the hats were driven insane by "Danbury disease." This also explains where the saying "mad as a hatter" comes from. (In this connection, it is important to know that liquid mercury, when swallowed, is unlikely to be absorbed into the body. Young babies who crawl on a floor where, for example, a mercury thermometer has been broken are at much greater risk from breathing the vapor of the metal.)

Thallium salts, which have been used in insecticides and depilatories (substances for removing hair, wool, or bristles), have also been employed for murder. In 1949, in Sydney, Australia, middle-aged Caroline Grills was found guilty of attempted murder with thallium. She was committed to prison for life, where the inmates called her "Aunt Thally." In 1971, in England, Graham Young killed two co-workers with a thallium compound used in the manufacture of photographic lenses.

DEADLY MEDICINE

During the 19th century, as the science of chemistry developed, chemists began to purify an increasing number of poisons for human consumption. Many of these became the stock-in-trade of pharmacists and found their way into the hands of murderers. And, not surprisingly, many cases involved those who had the easiest access to poisons—members of the medical profession. Today, the development of drugs for specific diseases has increased the number of poisons available to many thousands, and most family medicine chests contain at least one fatal drug.

Nobody will ever know how many deaths, certified as "natural" by the patient's physician, have been, in fact, cases of murder—or, at best, **euthanasia**. The most notorious killing spree in recent years was that of Dr. Harold Shipman in England.

Imprisoned for life in 2000 for the murder of 15 of his women patients with morphine, he has since been suspected of as many as 600 deaths. It was calculated that at the height of his career, he was killing an average of

In Britain, the Arsenic Act of 1851, and subsequent legislation, made it much harder for poisoners to commit murder without detection. Two years before the passing of the Act, this cartoon in the magazine *Punch* satirized the ease with which poison could be bought, even by young children.

Members of the medical profession have ready access to a wide range of poisonous drugs. The English physician Dr. Harold Shipman, who may have murdered as many as 600 of his patients, made out prescriptions for diamorphine, and stockpiled the drug for his purposes.

four or five patients each month.

Medical workers in hospitals and retirement homes have also been involved in cases of poisoning of their patients. One of the worst cases of recent years was that of Genene Jones, who was a respected, hard-working, children's nurse in San Antonio, Texas. Whenever a youngster suffered sudden cardiac arrest while in her care, the thrill of resuscitating him or her caused her great excitement. Her excitement was so great, in fact, that she injected near-lethal drugs into them in order to experience the thrill of nursing them back to life.

The drug that Genene favored was succinylcholine, also known as "synthetic **curare**," and it was the discovery of vials she had tampered with that eventually led to her detection. This drug—like the curare that South American native people apply to the tips of their arrows—relaxes and then paralyzes muscle fiber, rendering the victim unable to breathe. In February 1984, Genene was found guilty of murder and sentenced to a minimum of 25 years imprisonment. She was probably responsible for the deaths of more than 30 young children in her care.

Genene suffered from a psychological condition known as Munchausen syndrome by proxy, and there have been a number of similar cases among medical personnel. In 1989, Richard Angelo, a male nurse at the Good Samaritan Hospital in West Islip, NY, was found guilty of injecting four patients with muscle relaxants. "I felt inadequate … I felt I had to prove myself," he said in a videotaped confession. In 1991, English nurse Beverley Allitt was found guilty on four charges of murder, and three of attempted murder, of children in her care. She had injected them with massive overdoses of insulin.

FATAL GAS

There are a number of poisonous gases, of which two are the most-often detected in cases of death: carbon monoxide and hydrogen cyanide. Both act by preventing oxygen from reaching the body tissues.

In the past, household coal gas was a ready source of carbon monoxide. It was a popular means of suicide, caused many deaths by accident, and was also used in a number of murders. Now, it has largely been replaced by natural gas, but carbon monoxide can still be produced by incomplete combustion of all fuels, including coal. Car exhaust systems not fitted with modern catalytic converters emit four to eight percent carbon monoxide, and an engine running in a closed garage can result in death within a few minutes. In fires, too, the inhalation of carbon monoxide is often the primary cause of death.

Because carbon monoxide is odorless and tasteless, the victim may be unaware of anything but a headache before falling unconscious. A sure sign of this kind of poisoning is the cherry-pink coloration of the skin, lips, and internal organs, and this is also noticeable in hypostasis. Analysis in the laboratory will confirm the presence of carbon monoxide in the blood.

Hydrogen cyanide is a gas with a characteristic smell of bitter almonds, and prussic acid is a solution of this gas in water. The salts of the acid, usually sodium cyanide or potassium cyanide, are white powders. Cyanides are widely used in industry and as **fumigants**, but as a cause of death, they are most often found in cases of suicide. Because of the small quantity needed and because antidotes must be given at once (and are seldom available), cyanide was the favorite poison in "suicide pills" issued to spies.

Modern advances in chemical warfare have resulted in the preparation of a range of "nerve gases," which block the transmission of nerve impulses from the brain to the rest of the body, rapidly resulting in death. On March 19, 1995, members of the Japanese Aum Shirikyo sect released the nerve gas sarin in the Tokyo subway, killing 12 people and resulting in 5,000 suffering from ill effects.

BIOLOGICAL AGENTS

Biological cultures have so far remained a rare means of homicidal poisoning. In 1910, Dr. Bennett Clarke Hyde was suspected of injecting typhoid

The release of sarin nerve gas in the Tokyo subway in 1995 highlighted the threat of similar terrorist activities. In a climate of heightened security, many authorities have carried out exercises to simulate a poison gas attack, as in this mock drill in the subway at Taipei, Taiwan.

The possibility of biological warfare has made the work of forensic investigators even more difficult. Scientists entering the Hart Senate Office Building on Capitol Hill in November 2001 wore biohazard suits and respirators to protect them against possible infection by anthrax.

bacteria into five victims, but this could not be proved. In 1916, New York dentist Arthur Waite admitted to killing his mother-in-law by adding diphtheria and influenza cultures to her food.

The most feared biological agent is anthrax. It is a bacillus (bacterium) that normally kills cattle and sheep, but it can form spores that will survive in dry conditions for 40 years or more. Apart from the fatalities that occurred during the fall of 2001, threats of anthrax contamination have been used in the United States on several occasions by right-wing activists and those opposed to pro-choice organizations.

DETECTING POISONS

The symptoms of murder by poison may be immediately obvious: sudden death for no apparent physical reason, contortion of the body, unusual appearance of the eyes, or skin discoloration. On the other hand, poisons can mimic, or accelerate, death from natural causes. Whenever a pathologist suspects poison in the body at autopsy, a toxicologist must search for any one of a vast range of possible substances.

Before reliable methods of chemical analysis became available, examiners were forced to rely on a highly dangerous method of identifying certain alkaloid drugs (a group that includes aconitine, nicotine, morphine, hyoscine, and strychnine)—their sense of taste.

For example, when the Comte de Bocarmé and his wife were accused of poisoning her brother with nicotine in 1850, Belgian chemist Jean Servais Stas made an extract from the dead man's organs and reported "a burning sensation" on his tongue when he tasted it. He subsequently confirmed his findings by killing two dogs with nicotine. In 1881, Englishman George Lamson was accused of murdering his wife's young brother with aconitine. Dr. Thomas Stevenson of Guy's Hospital, London, prepared a similar extract: "Some of this extract I placed on my tongue," he said in evidence, "and it produced the effect of aconitia."

Poisoning by strychnine, on the other hand, produces immediate dramatic symptoms. The victim's muscles go into spasm; the back arches, so that only the head and heels touch the surface on which he or she is lying; and the mouth reveals a hideous grinning known as *risus sardonicus*. Nevertheless, examining physicians have sometimes failed to observe these ominous signs. When Dr. Thomas Neill Cream poisoned a series of prostitutes with strychnine in London in 1891–1892, the death of at least one was attributed to alcoholism.

The detection of arsenic was made possible by the Marsh test, which has since been superseded by even more delicate tests. Gradually, chemical analysis methods have been developed for all the elements, mostly metallic, which can cause death by poison. In a modern laboratory, a bank of computer-controlled instruments automatically conducts systematic analysis of this kind. Elements can also be identified by the specific wavelengths of light they produce when heated to a high temperature.

Instruments that employ this technique are known as **spectrometers**. There is also a wide range of "spot tests" for specific poisons, which produce either a colored reaction or the formation of characteristic crystals that can be examined further.

Mixtures of organic substances (materials derived from plants and animals, or drug capsules) have to be separated into their basic components. The simplest method of doing this is by chromatography. The technique used depends upon the degree to which the different components become dissolved in a current of either a liquid or a gas, so that they are gradually separated. They emerge from the analyzing instrument, one after the other, and can then be detected in a variety of ways. Gas chromatography can also be used in the analysis of solid materials, such as fiber or glass fragments, which are heated until they vaporize.

Another technique is **electrophoresis**, whereby the components are separated by the rates at which they move across an electrical field. Further details of this method will be found in Chapter Four.

Two of the more modern analytical techniques are mass spectrometry

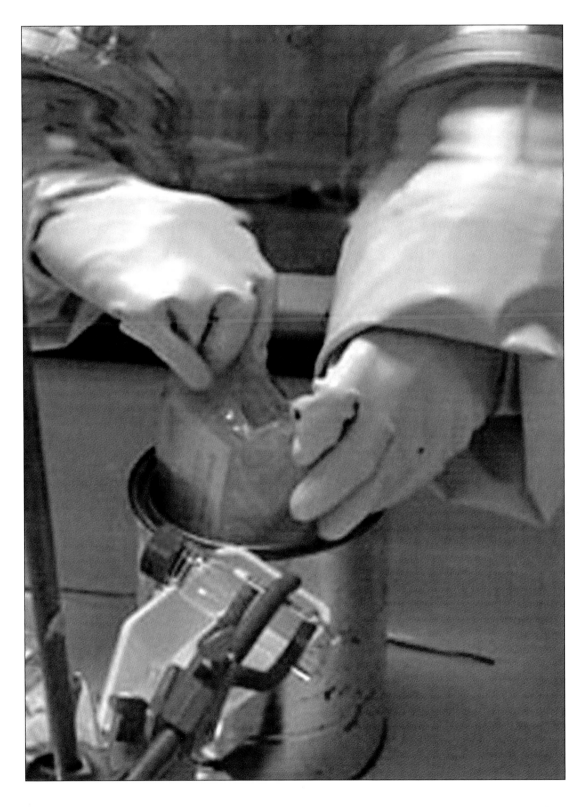

FBI scientists began the process of opening an anthrax-laden letter sent to Vermont Democratic Senator Patrick Leahy in October 2001, hoping to find clues to help identify the source of germ attacks. It is estimated that the letter could contain enough spores to kill 100,000 people.

THE WIZARD OF BERKELEY

Eva Rablen poisoned her husband Carroll with strychnine at a dance in Tuttletown, California, on April 29, 1929. His death was at first believed to be due to natural causes, but a detailed search of the premises eventually uncovered a hidden bottle of the drug, and further analysis revealed traces in Carroll's body.

There was still no direct way to connect Eva Rablen with the poisoning, and the prosecution sought the services of an independent forensic scientist, Dr. Edward Heinrich, who was known as the "wizard of Berkeley" because of his many successes in forensic investigations. It was suspected that the strychnine had been in a cup of coffee that Eva had given Carroll immediately before his death, and Heinrich reasoned that she might have spilt a little while crossing the crowded dance floor. He found a young woman who remembered Eva spilling coffee on her, and her stained dress revealed traces of the poison. Recognizing Heinrich's formidable reputation, Eva pleaded guilty in order to avoid the death penalty.

and neutron activation. A mass spectrometer analyzes an organic compound in terms of its constituent parts, and is particularly valuable when very small quantities are present. In neutron activation, the elements present are bombarded with neutrons in the core of a nuclear reactor. This causes each element to emit gamma rays of a distinguishing energy level.

In spite of all these technological developments, there are still cases in which laboratory mice must be used to compare the effect of a suspected poison with a known substance. When English hospital worker Kenneth Barlow killed his wife with two injections of insulin in 1957, he thought the crime was undetectable because insulin is produced naturally in the body by the pancreas. However, a minute examination of Mrs. Barlow's corpse revealed the tiny marks of the injections, and samples of the skin, fat, and muscle in the area were taken. The total weight of the tissue was only six ounces, but, in a set of control experiments, extracts were injected into laboratory mice. The results indicated that there was more insulin in the tissue samples than would normally have been found in Mrs. Barlow's entire body.

Rapid developments are being made in laboratory analytical instruments. A groundbreaking mass spectrometry technique at Manchester Metropolitan University, England, takes a "mass fingerprint" of unidentified bacteria, and matches it against a database in seconds.

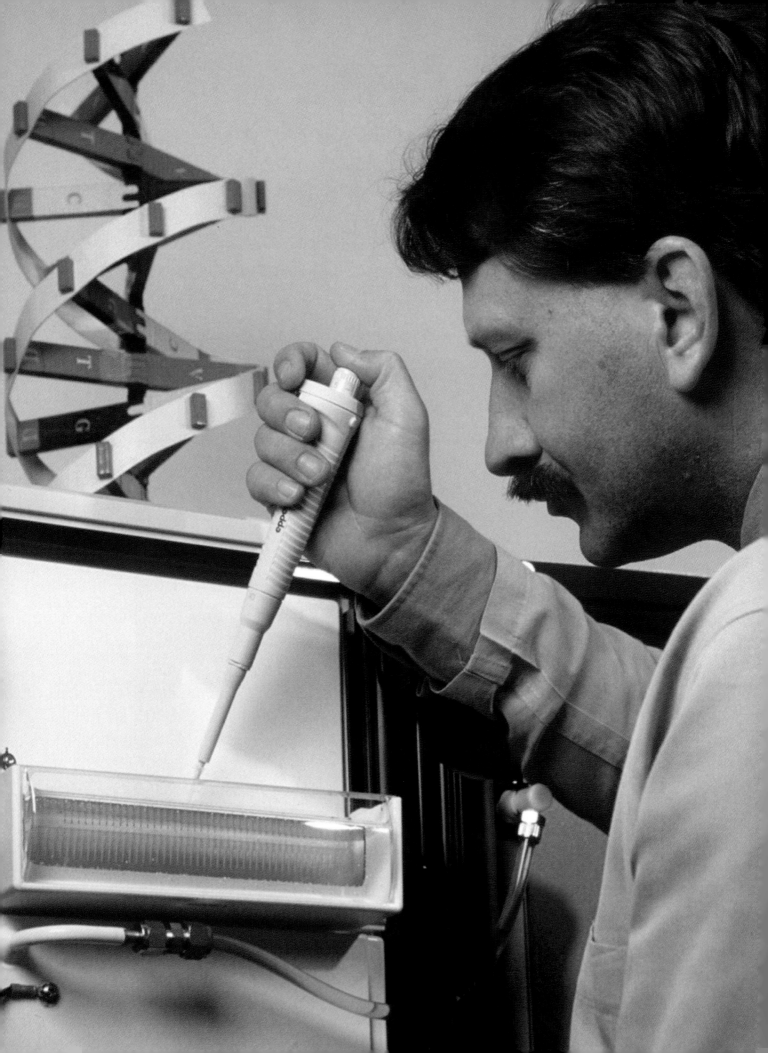

Telltale Blood

At the scene of any violent crime, the examining officer is likely to find blood and traces of other bodily fluids. These can tell a great deal about what occurred, not only about how the crime was committed, but also about the persons involved.

These days, nearly everybody knows his or her basic blood type, whether it is A, B, AB, or O, and Rhesus negative or positive. This division of blood into types was first made by Austrian physiologist Karl Landsteiner at the end of the 19th century. In his experiments, he took samples of blood and separated the red cells from the liquid, called the serum. He achieved this by spinning the blood at high speed in a centrifuge. Then he took the serum and added red cells from different people. They behaved in two different ways: either the cells mixed with the serum, or they clumped together ("agglutinated").

Numerous attempts at blood transfusion had been made in the past, but this observation explained for the first time why so many had failed. If the blood was not of the same type as that in the body, it produced clotting, and the patient died. Quick tests of blood samples to discover whether agglutination occurs must now be made before a transfusion is performed.

DIVIDING BLOOD INTO GROUPS

Red blood cells carry substances called antigens. These help make antibodies that fight infection and disease. Landsteiner suggested that his experiment showed the presence of two specific antigens, which he labeled A and

Left: Here, FBI agent Mark Wilson loads DNA material onto a DNA sequencer to carry out tests that may match the DNA of a suspect with material evidence from a crime scene. DNA material is relatively easy to extract from human tissue, such as blood, fingernails, skin, and saliva.

Karl Landsteiner began his investigation into blood groups in Austria, toward the end of the 19th century. His discoveries were important: not only did they make it possible to distinguish persons with different blood types, they also made safe blood transfusion possible.

B. The discovery of these antigens enabled him to divide human blood into four basic groups:

Group A: antigen A present; antigen B absent
Group B: antigen A absent; antigen B present
Group AB: both antigens A and B present
Group O: both antigens absent

The particular blood group of an individual depends on the genetic inheritance from both parents. Known as ABO typing, it has been used, for example, to help identify the biological father in a paternity case. How common each group is can vary from one national population to another. In the United States, for example, the relative proportions of ABO groups are roughly 39 percent A, 13 percent B, 43 percent O, and 5 percent AB.

In 1927, Landsteiner discovered two other antigen types, labeling their occurrence as M, N, and MN. In 1940, working in the United States, he and A.S. Wiener discovered the Rhesus factor, named after the Rhesus monkeys they investigated. Since then, other researchers have introduced more than a dozen additional group systems. Different proteins and enzymes associated with specific blood groups have also been identified.

WHAT THIS MEANS FOR FORENSICS

The ability to identify blood type is a powerful tool for uncovering crucial evidence in a forensic investigation. If, for example, a victim's ABO type is O, and bloodstains of this type are found on the clothing of a suspect whose type is A, there is a likely probability that they have come from the victim.

Making use of the many other blood type systems now available, this probability can be greatly increased. If blood of type O occurs in 43 percent of the population, the substance haptoglobin-2 in 36 percent of these, and the enzyme PGM-2 in five percent, then the probability of an individual having these three blood types together is 43 x 36 x 5 = 7,740 in

Blood is one of the most valuable sources of evidence for the forensic scientist. ABO grouping and DNA typing can help the investigator to identify a mutilated victim, and also narrow down the list of suspects, sometimes to a single perpetrator.

IS IT HUMAN BLOOD?

When dark-red stains are found at the crime scene, the first question to be decided is whether or not they are bloodstains. Police officers have sometimes jumped to the wrong conclusion and launched a murder hunt for a nonexistent victim. Simple chemical tests in the laboratory can quickly distinguish blood from other substances.

The next question is whether this is human blood or that of some other animal. A century ago, German biologist Paul Uhlenhuth found that serum from one species would cause blood from another species to form a cloudy precipitate ("precipitin") in a manner similar to the way red blood cells agglutinated (clumped together). With a range of serums from specific animals available, an analyst can quickly determine what species blood comes from.

Within weeks of his discovery, Uhlenhuth was able to detect both human and sheep's blood on the clothing of a German, Ludwig Tessnow. Labeled the "Mad Carpenter," Tessnow was accused of killing several young people and slaughtering a farmer's sheep. Tessnow was convicted and executed in 1904.

1,000,000. In other words, around eight people in every 1,000 will have this specific type of blood. It is still insufficient to obtain a conviction on this evidence alone, but it can help to narrow the number of suspects.

In 1925, another valuable discovery was made. Around 80 percent of humans are "secretors." This means their saliva, urine, perspiration, and semen contain the same substances as their blood, and can be used for typing in much the same way. In 1940, two British researchers found that it was possible to distinguish between female and male body cells, particularly the white blood cells and those of the lining of the mouth. Blood typing has now become so precise that recently, one scientist showed that he could distinguish between the blood of his twin daughters, who were genetically identical, because one had suffered from chicken pox and the other had not.

SPLASHES OF BLOOD

At the scene of a violent homicidal attack, blood may be present in considerable quantities. Not only will it be found on the victim, but also on the weapon and the surroundings. Indoors, the floors, walls, and even the ceilings may be splashed. Careful observation of these bloodstains can provide valuable clues about what took place. Bloodstains and splashes are classified into six basic types.

Round drops are found on horizontal surfaces; depending on the height from which they fell, they can spray out into a starlike shape. Splashes of blood are shaped like an exclamation mark; they show that blood has flown through the air and hit a surface at an angle. While a victim is still alive, spurts of blood come from the pumping action of the heart. A major artery or vein can spray the blood a considerable distance.

Pools form around the body of the bleeding victim. If there is more than one pool, he either dragged himself, or was moved, from one spot to another before dying. Smears are likely also found in this case. Trails are left when a bloody corpse is moved. There will be drops if the body was carried, and smears if it was dragged.

The importance of bloodstains was shown in the case of English farmer Graham Backhouse in 1984. He was found standing in his kitchen, covered in blood, with deep slashes across his face and chest. Down the hallway, his neighbor lay shot, with a craft knife in his hand. Backhouse said the neighbor had attacked him with the knife; they had struggled, and he had shot the man in self defense.

However, many of the blood drops on the kitchen floor were round, indicating that Backhouse bled standing still, and some kitchen chairs had

The shape of drops of free blood on nearby surfaces can tell the investigator much about the circumstances in which they were formed. They may indicate the type of attack made against the victim, and also whether the body was then moved, as well as how.

Here, Hugo Jorquera, head of the DNA unit in Santiago, Chile, tests blood samples taken from the family members of those who disappeared during Augusto Pinochet's dictatorship in the 1970s. Many bodies were found in mass graves, and blood typing may help establish their identities.

A forensic scientist removes samples of dried blood for analysis from the blade of a knife used in a homicidal attack. Liquid blood deteriorates rapidly, and even blood-soaked articles should be allowed to dry as quickly as possible.

been toppled on top of the spots. One of them had a smear of his blood on its back, but there was no blood on the gun. Adding up the evidence provided by the bloodstains, it became obvious that Backhouse had slashed himself with the knife after shooting his unsuspecting neighbor.

DNA "FINGERPRINTING"

Blood typing is still sometimes used in the simpler cases, such as that of Graham Backhouse. For more complicated cases, however, DNA typing is the preferred method for investigation. Exaggerated claims were made for it during its early development, but a sufficiently careful analysis can now identify an individual as concretely as a fingerprint. And unlike identification of a fingerprint, which must be substantially complete, DNA analysis requires only a few body cells. DNA stands for deoxyribonucleic acid, which is the genetic material of all the cells of the body containing a nucleus: tissues, bone marrow, hair, tooth pulp, semen, and white blood cells, as well as waste cells in saliva and urine. Red blood cells, however, do not have a nucleus, so they cannot be used in DNA analysis.

The shape of the DNA molecule is like a long ladder twisted into a tight helix. The two sides of the ladder are made up of alternating groups of phosphate and the sugar deoxyribose; and the "rungs" of the ladder are formed of two purine bases joined at each side to a sugar molecule.

When a cell divides—as the human fetus develops, as the body later grows, and throughout life—the ladder separates down its length into two single strands, each half then becoming a model for the formation of a new DNA molecule. Short sections of the ladder make up the genes, which determine inherited characteristics, such as eye and skin color, blood type, and so on. No two people—except twins who develop from a single egg— are identical; they differ in the combination of their genes.

Enzymes are substances that control the thousands of complex chemical processes that go on in the body. Biologists discovered that certain enzymes produced by bacteria cut up the DNA into sections. Known as "restriction enzymes," bacteria use these to protect themselves against viruses by attacking any "foreign" DNA. So far, more than 400 restriction enzymes have been isolated. Each one will cut human DNA at a different place.

It is a relatively simple matter to extract DNA from body cells and treat it with one or more of these specific enzymes. The different fragments of the ladder that are produced vary in length according to the structure of the individual's DNA. This means they have different molecular sizes and can be separated by electrophoresis.

A way of detecting the separated fragments was developed by American scientist Edwin Southern in 1975, and is known as the "Southern blot." The electrophoresis gel is soaked in a solution that halves the fragments into two strands, and these are "blotted" off onto a plastic membrane. The

ELECTROPHORESIS

Electrophoresis involves taking a glass plate coated with gel and applying a low-voltage electric current directly across it. The sample containing the DNA fragments is placed at the negative end of the plate, and the molecules move across the gel toward the positive end at different speeds according to their size. Since they move directly in a straight line, it is possible to place a number of samples side by side for comparison. After several hours, the fragments will have separated across the plate.

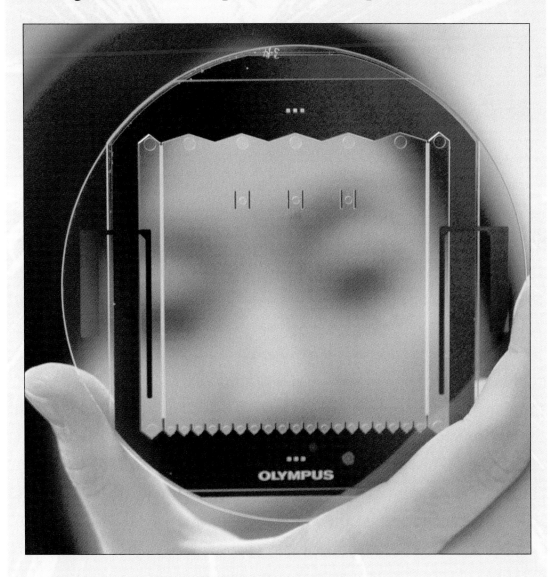

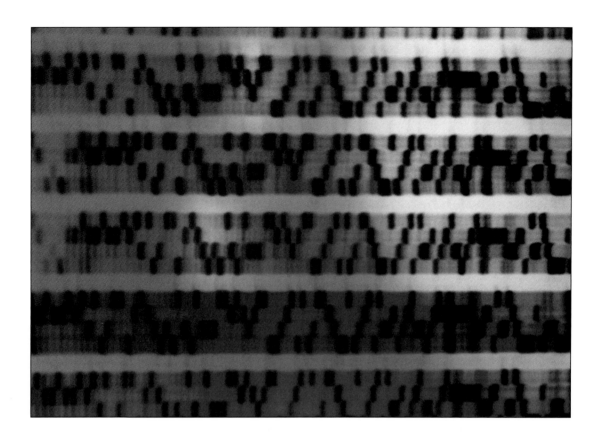

An "autoradiograph" of separated DNA fragments is made up of short, dark bands, similar to a bar code. Bands that are level with one another across the film indicate fragments that are of the same structure.

membrane is then treated with one or more "probes." A probe is a short length of single-strand DNA that has been separately prepared and "labeled" with a radioactive atom. Each probe finds a matching group in the single-strand fragments and attaches to it in the same way in which new double-stranded DNA is formed in dividing cells.

When the membrane is placed in contact with a sheet of x-ray photographic film, the radioactivity produces an image. The result is an "autoradiograph" of short, dark bands across the film, not unlike the bar codes that are read at checkouts. Bands that are level with one another across the film indicate molecules of the same structure—that is, matching fragments.

In many cases, the sample of DNA that can be obtained from a crime scene is quite small. A technique known as PCR has now been developed.

It uses an enzyme that copies a DNA strand; this produces two strands, each of which is copied, which produce two more strands, and so on in a chain reaction, so that a million or more copies can be made in a short time. This method has its limitations, however; each enzyme will copy only a specific fragment, so few different fragments can be distinguished.

DNA DATABASES

Since 1998, local, state, and federal agencies have been building DNA databases, which can be consulted the same way as fingerprint records. To match a sample, however, you need to know how frequently the identifiable fragment occurs in the general population. For example, suppose three fragments have been identified, with relative frequencies of 42, 32, and one in 100. The probability that all three will appear in a single sample is 42 x 32 x 1 = 1,344 in one million, or approximately 1 in 744—and even a small-town population is bigger than that. This is why prosecuting counsel must be careful when arguing that two samples come from the same person. In more than one case, DNA evidence has been disallowed when counsel showed the prosecution did not have a thorough understanding of the numbers involved. DNA typing of this kind must, therefore, be treated with caution, although there have been many successes. In Britain, a more time-consuming technique was the method first developed in 1984 by Alex Jeffreys, who gave it the name "DNA fingerprinting." He has claimed that using this technique, the chance that two people (other than twins) will have the same pattern of fragments is less than 1 in 1,000,000,000,000,000,000,000,000,000,000. This figure is billions of times greater than the population of the world.

The Human Genome Project was begun in 1988, and researchers all over the world have contributed to the identification of every gene in human DNA. Once the work is complete, police authorities believe they will be able to provide a full physical description of a wanted person from analysis of his or her DNA.

The Smoking Gun

With the exception of smoothbore shotguns, most guns manufactured since the early 19th century have had rifled barrels. Spiral grooves cut along the inside of the barrel cause the bullet to spin and give greater accuracy of aim. The uncut parts of the barrel between the grooves are called "lands." To ensure a tight fit, bullets are made slightly larger than the barrel. As a result, these lands will produce clearly visible grooves along the length of the bullet.

This is the basis of the forensic science of ballistics, and the first murder case in which the identification of these grooves was made occurred more than a century ago. In 1889, Alexander Lassagne, Professor of Forensic Medicine at Lyon University, France, matched seven grooves found on a bullet recovered from a victim's body with seven **rifling** grooves in a gun in possession of a suspect.

Every gun manufacturer uses a distinctive type of rifling, and a firearms examiner can quickly discover the make of a gun from the number of grooves, the relative width of grooves and **lands**, and whether the rifling is left-handed or right-handed. However, there is more to ballistics examination than this. Because each gun is rifled on the same machine, the tools become slightly worn, or even damaged. The pattern of the groove changes, and there may also be slight scratches (striations) on the bullet, parallel to the grooves. Careful examination of the grooves and striations under a microscope can make it possible to identify an individual gun as the one that fired the bullet.

Left: A police investigator examines a bullet hole in a window of a building in the financial district of Manila, the Philippines. The size and shape of the hole, and the cracks radiating from it, can help provide information on the bullet's velocity, and the distance from which it was fired.

On December 30, 1999, a man armed with two automatic handguns killed four people in the lobby of a hotel in Tampa, Florida. He then fled, hijacking a car and killing the woman driver. However, he left this gun in the car; a police expert, wearing latex gloves, is putting it into a paper evidence sack.

Although careful criminals—knowing the skills of ballistics examiners—will try to collect them and carry them away, spent cartridge cases may be found at the scene of a crime where firearms were used. These cartridge cases can provide valuable evidence. When a gun is fired, the pressure drives the cartridge case against the hardened steel of the **breechblock**. Any slight marking of the block will leave its imprint on the softer metal of the cap of the case, and the firing pin will also leave its own print on the cap. If the gun is automatic or semiautomatic, the ejector mechanism is also likely to leave characteristic marks on the case. The ballistics examiner will discover all these marks.

In 1900, Dr. A. Llewellyn Hall published his book *The Missile and the Weapon*, in which he described the principles of firearm identification. The book attracted the attention of the famous jurist Oliver Wendell Holmes, and two years later, he heard the trial of a man named Best accused of murder with a revolver. Holmes consulted a gunsmith, who fired a bullet from Best's gun into a box of wadded cotton batting. In court, using a magnifying glass, the gunsmith demonstrated the points of similarity between the two bullets to the jury, and a conviction was secured. Today, because the fibers of the cotton may leave marks on the bullet, the test shots are fired into a water tank where six feet of water is sufficient to stop the bullet.

BALLISTICS COMES OF AGE

The establishment of forensic ballistics in the United States owes much to the work of Charles Waite, who was an assistant in the office of the New York State Prosecutor. In 1915, a man named Stielow was found guilty of a double shooting and sent to Sing Sing to await the electric chair. His attorneys obtained a stay of execution, and soon after, two vagrants confessed to the murder. Waite had Stielow's gun and bullets examined. The grooves left by the lands were not similar at all, and Stielow then obtained a pardon.

SACCO AND VANZETTI

In 1920, Nicolo Sacco and Bartolomeo Vanzetti were charged with murder during a payroll robbery in South Braintree, Massachusetts. At their trial the following year, one prosecution witness testified that Sacco's gun had fired the fatal shots, but this was contested by two defense experts, James Burns and Augustus Gill. When both men were declared guilty and sentenced to death, there were protests from all over the world, and the execution was stayed for several years.

Following this, Waite spent two years traveling the United States and Europe, collecting data from every firearms manufacturer. This soon led to his appointment as head of the Bureau of Forensic Ballistics in New York, the first of its kind in the world. When Waite died in 1926, his successor was Colonel Calvin Goddard. An important development at this time was the invention of the comparison microscope. This consists of two microscope objectives with a single eyepiece. When a bullet is placed under each objective, the marks on each can be compared directly. One of Goddard's first major cases in which he used this instrument, was that of Sacco and Vanzetti (see page 67).

In 1927, Colonel Goddard offered his services as an unbiased expert in this case. In Gill's presence, he fired a shot from Sacco's gun, and then placed it beside the fatal bullet under the comparison microscope. The bullets matched. As there was no further hope for Sacco and Vanzetti, they were sentenced to death and went to the electric chair.

The controversy continued, however. In 1961, a forensic team led by Colonel Frank Jury, former head of the New Jersey Firearms Laboratory, declared that the bullet had indeed come from Sacco's gun. Finally, in 1983, another team, financed by a Boston television station, confirmed Goddard's original finding.

IDENTIFICATION GAINS SOPHISTICATION

In 1929, Goddard was able to identify two Thompson submachine guns used in the infamous Saint Valentine's Day Massacre on February 14, 1929, when members of Al Capone's gang slaughtered six of George "Bugs" Moran's men in Chicago. J. Edgar Hoover, director of the recently formed FBI, was so impressed that he persuaded Goddard to found the Scientific Crime Detection Laboratory at Northwestern University in Evanston, Illinois. Soon after, Hoover set up the FBI Ballistics Department in Washington, D.C., which is now the largest firearms investigation center in the world.

While bystanders gather around, a Mexican policeman picks up one of the shell casings at the scene of the assassination of two of President Zedillo's bodyguards in 1999. This is bad forensic practice, since the crime scene should be immediately sealed-off and forensic experts allowed to examine the area for evidence.

On February 14, 1929, five men, disguised as police officers, entered the Chicago headquarters of "Bugs" Moran, a gangster rival of Al Capone. Armed with Tommy guns, they slaughtered six of Moran's men, together with a man who had only dropped by for a game of cards.

In Britain, gunsmith Robert Churchill had been appearing as an expert witness since 1912. In 1928, he traveled to meet Colonel Goddard and learn details of the comparison microscope. On his return, Churchill had an instrument made and achieved his first success in the case of two men accused of shooting a police constable. He and a team of three from the War Office reported that they had test-fired 1,300 revolvers without finding a ballistics match with the murder weapon. This case, together with that of Sacco and Vanzetti, attracted international attention. As a consequence, ballistics laboratories were set up in France, Germany, Norway, and Russia.

GUNSHOT WOUNDS

Close examination of the wound caused by a bullet can provide additional evidence. When a gun is fired at close range, particles of gunpowder produce a characteristic "tattooing" on exposed skin, or a similar pattern on clothing. This deposit, and its size, can give an indication of the direction and distance from which the weapon was fired. However, if the gun is held in contact with the skin, the powder pattern is usually absent; the same is true of shots from a distance greater than 10 feet.

A bullet will also leave minute traces of lead around the hole it makes, which can be detected by chemical analysis. It will pick up traces of anything it passes through, or ricochets from, and fragments of bone, hair, building materials, paint, glass, fibers, or even blood can be detected. This

BLOWBACK

When a suspect is detained in a shooting incident, his or her hands are customarily examined. The rapid expansion of the explosion in a gun barrel is followed by "blowback," and residues, which can be removed by swabbing, will likely be found on the hands of the shooter. Formerly, the swab was tested for nitrates, which are found in explosive residues. However, nitrates are increasingly used in cigarettes and cosmetics, as well as in agricultural chemicals and drugs for the treatment of heart conditions, so other tests are now used. Barium and antimony from the primer, for example, leave microscopic particles that can be detected and analyzed.

Blowback can also draw material from the surroundings into the gun barrel. In one murder case, the killer held a pillow over the muzzle of the gun to muffle the noise of the shot. Fragments of a feather were later found in a suspect's weapon.

can be very important in calculating the path of the bullet.

In examining a dead body, the pathologist will trace the path of a bullet through the tissues. A spinning bullet leaves a rifled barrel at over 1,500 feet per second; but soon it starts to develop "tail wag" and begins to wobble in its flight. At close range, the entry wound may be a small hole, approximately the same size of the bullet; but, if it is already wagging when it makes contact, the bullet can produce a large, lacerated wound. Within the body, the force of the bullet causes the tissues to expand and then collapse in on themselves, leaving a clearly defined track.

THE UNEXPECTED BEHAVIOR OF BULLETS

This track can sometimes show the bullet traveling in strange, unexpected ways. The Scottish pathologist Sir Sydney Smith described a case in which a soldier was shot. The bullet entered the outer side of his left thigh, leaving a small entrance wound. It then passed out and into the right thigh, where it disintegrated, a fragment causing what at first looked like an entrance wound in the outside of the right thigh. "Anyone without experience...," wrote Smith, "might, on looking at the wounds, have assumed that two shots had been fired, one from the left and the other from the right."

The FBI has come across similar bizarre incidents. In one, the victim was hit in the wrist with a .22-**caliber** bullet. This caliber was small enough to travel up a vein in his arm and into his heart, killing him.

In another case, a gunman held up a bank in Oklahoma, but was recognized by the teller, a girl who had been at school with him. He took her and two other witnesses behind the bank, where he shot them and left them for dead. In the teller's case, the bullet entered her skull, traveled round inside it, and exited from her forehead. She fell unconscious, but her brain was undamaged, and in due course, she was able to testify against the gunman.

High-velocity bullets can travel long distances in a straight line, and sometimes it is possible to discover where they were fired. One day, a bullet came through a window and into the wall of the Israeli Consulate in

Washington, D.C., and at first, it was supposed to be a terrorist attack. FBI agents aimed a laser beam from the impact point on the wall through the hole in the window. It passed between nearby buildings and indicated an open area several blocks away. They found that a security guard had been chasing a handbag thief and had fired a shot at him. Ballistics examination showed that the bullet had come from the guard's gun.

When John Hinckley shot President Ronald Reagan in 1981, FBI experts had difficulty in accounting for all the bullets. They knew that six

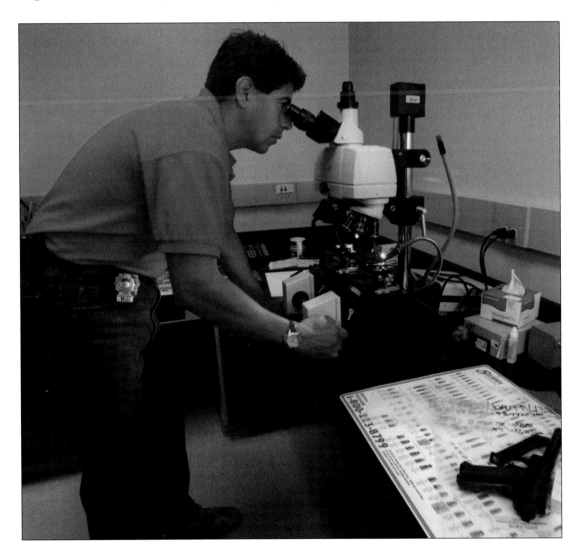

At the FBI Forensic Science Research and Training Center at Quantico, Virginia, a detective from the Syracuse NY Police Department gains experience in using a comparison microscope. The instrument enables the markings on two bullets or casings to be examined together and matched.

shots had been fired: The wounded victims accounted for four, and the fifth had hit the rear window of the limousine. A detailed search was mounted around the scene, but it was some time before the remains of the sixth bullet were found. It had struck a window across the street, leaving only a small hole in the glass, and had then fallen in fragments to the floor.

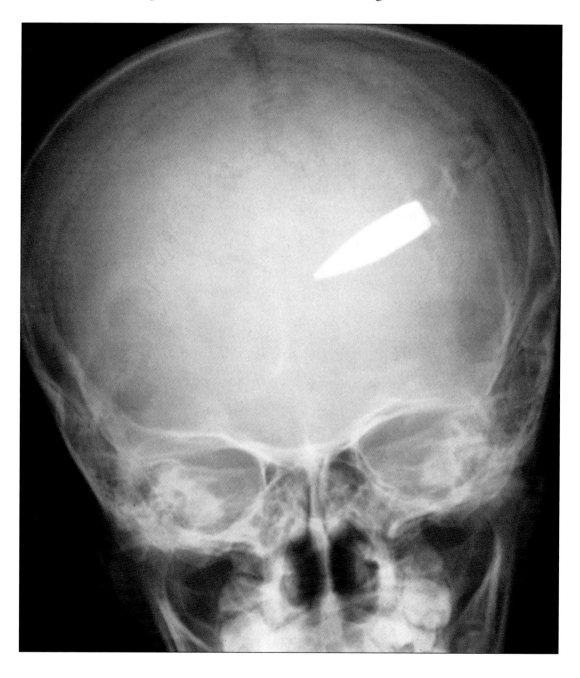

An x-ray shows a bullet lodged in the skull of a victim of a shooting. The position and depth of the bullet will help forensic experts establish the trajectory and distance from which it was fired.

THE ASSASSINATION OF PRESIDENT KENNEDY

Following the shooting of John F. Kennedy in Dallas, Texas, on November 22, 1963, there was a long-running argument about the number of shots that had been fired. None of the pathologists who examined the  President's body had much experience with gunshot wounds, and the Warren Commission, set up in 1964 to examine the evidence, did not interview a single forensic expert. It was not until 1977 that the Congress Select Committee on Assassinations assembled a panel of forensic pathologists, headed by Dr. Michael Baden, the New York City Medical Examiner.

The panel found that a tracheotomy had been performed on the President's throat in an attempt to allow him to breathe, and that this had obscured the exit wound of the bullet that struck him in the back. This bullet had then hit Governor Connally in the back sideways on, leaving an entry wound two inches long, exited below his right nipple, entered his right wrist, and finally passed through part of his left thigh. It was found lying on the stretcher that carried Connally to the hospital.

Enhanced prints of x-rays showed that a second bullet had struck the President in the head and exited above his right ear. It struck the windscreen pillar of the car, and was eventually found on the floor. Dr. Baden and his colleagues were convinced there had been only two shots and that both had come from behind.

Fragments of Evidence

At a crime scene, the forensic examiner searches for the tiniest scrap of "foreign" material—anything that may have been brought or left there by the criminal or the victim. Traces of hair, dirt, or fibers can indicate where the victim was before the crime or lead to the previous whereabouts of the criminal.

When suspects are apprehended, every item of their clothing and possessions, as well as their home and work environments, must be searched for similar trace evidence. If a vehicle has been used during a crime, it may have left, in addition to tire tracks, a minute scrape of paint on a tree or a wall. In a case of a hit-and-run offense, there are also likely to be fragments of glass or plastic.

Major forensic laboratories throughout the world keep thousands of samples of paper, fabrics, fibers and hairs, paints, glass, and other materials, together with databases of the physical properties of many more, and details provided by manufacturers. In the United States, for example, the National Automotive Paint File includes samples of more than 40,000 paint finishes. With access to information like this, together with the results of analysis, a forensic scientist can identify the make, model, and frequently even the year, of a car from a tiny chip of paint.

It is often possible to narrow this investigation even further. Eight or more layers of paint will be applied to a car during its manufacture, and examination of the chip under the microscope will reveal the color of these undercoats along its edge. In consultation with the manufacturers, this can

Left: Police in Northern Ireland search the ground for evidence after an Irish Republican Army (IRA) bomb blast. In the initial stages of a criminal investigation, police often carry out painstaking "fingertip" searches for any fragmentary evidence.

indicate the plant from which the car came and the period during which it was painted. The manufacturers will probably even be able to provide details of the dealers to whom a particular production batch of cars were delivered. And this can lead to identification of the car's owner.

HAIRS AND FIBERS

Some of the most significant traces left at a crime scene can be human or animal hairs or fibers from clothing, carpets, blankets, cord, rope, sacking, and many other materials.

Human hair is easily distinguished from animal hair. Examination under a microscope will show whether two human hairs are similar, but this is not sufficient to establish that they are identical, and DNA analysis must be used. Previously, it was necessary to find particles of tissue adhering to the root, but it is now possible to extract DNA even from cut or fallen hair. Neutron activation analysis (see Chapter 4) will establish which chemicals are in the hair, and it has been claimed that the chance of sample hairs from two sources exactly matching in their chemical composition is around one in a million.

Fabrics shed fibers constantly and also pick up "foreign" fibers on contact. When a fiber is discovered at a crime scene, the first step is to identify it. Is it a natural material, such as wool, silk, or cotton, or is it a manmade fiber? Artificial fibers are easy to distinguish from natural ones. They are smoother and have little or no internal structure. With a database of manufacturers to refer to, a forensic scientist can identify a particular manmade fiber and pinpoint who made it.

THE UNIQUE PROPERTIES OF GLASS

Glass is an unusual material. It is not a solid, but a liquid that is supercooled between two highly stressed "skins." This accounts both for its transparency and its tendency to shatter into tiny pieces. These two properties are of great value to the forensic scientist.

The remains of a baggage container, carried aboard PanAm flight 103A, which exploded above Lockerbie, Scotland, on December 21, 1988. Forensic experts were able to piece together fragments of a suitcase, the clothing in it, and the timing device that set off the explosion.

When a criminal breaks a pane of glass in a window or door, tiny pieces will nearly always be found in his or her clothing. Although most of the glass will fly away from the impact, up to 30 percent will fly toward the striker. The same is true if a bullet shatters a pane of glass. Tiny particles can travel as far as 18 feet toward the shooter.

It is up to the forensic scientist to prove that the fragments found in a suspect's clothing are of the same glass as that found at the crime scene. Many different types of glass are manufactured, but each has a specific **refractive index**, which can be measured in a tiny fragment. The density of the glass—its weight per cubic centimeter—can also be found by discovering whether it sinks, floats, or remains suspended in a range of liquids of known density. These findings can then be compared with manufacturers' data. Neutron activation analysis will identify the constituents in a speck of glass no bigger than a period.

If a car headlight or side-view mirror has been smashed, as frequently happens in hit-and-run incidents, the larger fragments must be painstakingly reassembled. It has proved possible to identify the make, and even the model of a particular car, by this means.

PAPER AND INK

Documents, both handwritten and printed, can provide all kinds of evidence in an investigation. Handwriting can reveal the personality and education of an individual, and can also be compared with that of a suspect. Many different kinds of ink can be analyzed, and the source of the paper determined.

A sheet of paper will often retain an indented impression of what had been written on the sheet on top of it, particularly if a ballpoint pen has been used. A recently developed technique is called the electrostatic detection apparatus, or ESDA. Pressure on the paper changes its electrical properties, and when it is treated with the powder from a photocopier, the indented image can be detected and read.

TELLTALE FIBERS

Between July 1979 and May 1981, more than 20 young African-American children and young men were found murdered on the outskirts of Atlanta, Georgia. Investigators found two types of fiber on their clothing: a yellowish-green nylon fiber that appeared to come from a carpet and violet acetate fibers. When 23-year-old Wayne Williams came under suspicion, police obtained a warrant to search his family's home. They found it carpeted throughout with an identical yellowish-green nylon.

This evidence in itself was insufficient, and the FBI was asked to investigate further. The type of nylon had been manufactured between 1967 and 1974 by a company in Boston, Massachusetts, and identification of the dye led to carpet manufacturers in Dalton, Georgia. They had used the fiber only through 1970–1971, but the yellowish-green carpet had been sold in 10 Southeastern states. Guessing that sales of this particular type of carpet had been fairly evenly distributed, and knowing the number of homes in Atlanta—nearly 640,000—the FBI calculated the chance that the fibers found on the victims came from the Williams' home could be reduced to one in some 8,000.

This was still not enough, but a search of Williams' car showed that its carpet matched a different fiber, rayon, found on one of the victims. Further inquiries by the FBI put the likelihood of this being a coincidence at one in over 3,000. Combining these two figures put the odds at one in 24 million. Violet acetate fibers were also found in the car and on a blanket in Williams' bedroom. When hairs from his dog also matched those found on several of the victims, the FBI was convinced of his guilt.

THE FBI LABORATORY

What was eventually to become the FBI Forensic Science Research and Training Center was first set up as a small laboratory on November 24, 1932. After being in several locations in central Washington, D.C., it was moved in 1981 to the Bureau's Academy in Quantico, Virginia. Now, more than one million examinations are conducted at the Center each year, and research into forensic casework and research is ongoing.

The Center also provides training—at no direct expense to state or local forensic laboratories—in latent fingerprint identification, DNA analysis, hair and fiber examination, bomb disposal, shoe- and tire-print analysis, and other techniques.

When baseball-wielding thugs attacked the offices of a Taiwanese magazine, they left the debris of a glass door shattered on the floor. However, many tiny fragments would have lodged in their clothing, and could be identified when they were later apprehended.

In every case of an unexplained fire, investigators have to seek evidence of a suspected arson attack. Here, in a burned-out Turkish shop in the city of Leipzig, Germany, police take photographs and gather up damaged fittings, in the expectation of finding traces of the cause.

FIRE AND EXPLOSION

Arson is the act of deliberately setting fire to another person's property or to one's own. It has been said, with some truth, that when trade is bad and businesses are failing, the number of arson cases increases. Investigation of arson involves three inquiries, which are largely independent of one another. Arson investigators need to know the cause of the fire; the police look for any perpetrator; and insurance investigators are anxious to discover any reason why compensation should not be paid.

The first essential piece is to discover where the fire started and when. The debris must be searched for signs that flammable material was piled up or a timing device used. If gasoline or another flammable liquid was used

WTC BOMBING

Before its destruction on September 11, 2001, the World Trade Center was the target of a previous terrorist attack. When an explosion ripped through its underground parking garage on February 26, 1993, FBI investigators were rapidly on the scene. Traces of a nitrate explosive were found over a wide area, and especially on the remains of a van. Mohammed Salameh had rented the van in Jersey City, and nitrate traces left by his hands were found on the rental agreement. Further inquiries led the FBI to Nidal Ayyad and Mahmud Abouhalima and the apartment in which they had made the explosive.

When an explosion rocked the Ministry of the Interior in central Rome, in February 2002, Italian police were swiftly on the scene. An investigator, in white coveralls and overshoes, searches among the debris, including a wrecked motorcycle, for traces of the bomb and its detonator.

to start the fire, traces will have soaked into charred wood or cracks in the structure, where they usually fail to burn from lack of oxygen. "Snifter" instruments can detect as little as 10 parts in a million of vapor, and gas **chromatography** in the forensic laboratory will identify the liquid that has been used.

Explosions must be investigated in much the same way. Criminal use of explosives occurs either in breaking and entering or in attacks against persons or property from either personal or political motives. An explosion investigator may also be called in for cases of fatal accident or suicide.

Unlike a fire, debris from an explosion will likely be scattered over a wide area, and every piece must be searched for evidence. The nature and

The clothing of both victim and suspect may be examined closely for traces of evidence. Here, a police laboratory technician in Totowa, New Jersey, extracts a bloodstain from a pair of jeans.

extent of the damage can indicate the site of the explosion and the direction in which the shock wave traveled. Fragments can reveal that a container was used and the material it was made out of. Pieces of a detonator, wires, or the fragments of a timing device may be found, and consulting manufacturers' data will often identify their source.

Nearly all explosives leave some solid residue as well as vapor, and samples of these can be analyzed chemically. Some of the chemicals that are used by manufacturers are also freely available as agricultural products and have been used in attacks by terrorist organizations. The bomb made by Timothy McVeigh and Terry Nichols to destroy the Alfred P. Murrah Federal Building in Oklahoma City on April 19, 1995, was one of these.

These, then, are just some of the many subtle investigative techniques available to the forensic scientist in the never-ending war against crime.

Fearsome destruction does not require the use of sophisticated explosives. A truck packed with diesel fuel and agricultural weedkiller exploded outside the Alfred P. Murrah Federal Building in Oklahoma City on April 19, 1995. It ripped open the side of the building, killing 168, many of them young children.

Shortly after the Oklahoma City bombing of 1995, 27-year-old Timothy McVeigh was arrested for a driving offense, and FBI inquiries soon implicated him and his accomplice Terry Nichols. McVeigh, a supporter of fundamentalist militia groups, claimed that the bombing was in retaliation for the death of 74 people at the Branch Davidian compound in Waco, Texas, two years earlier.

GLOSSARY

Anthropologist: a person who studies human beings in relation to distribution, origin, classification, and relationship of races, physical character, environmental and social relations, and culture

Asphyxiation: death by lack of oxygen or obstruction to normal breathing

Ballistics: the investigation of guns and bullets

Breechblock: the hardened steel "back" of the interior of a gun, through which the firing pin strikes the ignition cap of the bullet

Caliber: the diameter of a bullet, which can be measured in tenths of an inch or in millimeters

Chromatography: analysis of a mixture into its components, by observing the different rates at which the various components move in a flow of liquid or gas

Cirrhosis: a disease of the liver, most often due to alcoholism

Corpuscles: living cells, for example, blood cells

Curare: a poisonous substance derived from a South American plant

Dactylography: the original name for the taking and analysis of fingerprints

Electrophoresis: analysis of a mixture, usually of proteins or protein-related compounds, by the different rates at which they move across a weak electric field

Euthanasia: the act of killing or permitting the death of hopelessly sick or injured individuals in a relatively painless way for reasons of mercy

Exhume: to take out of a grave or tomb

Fumigant: a smoke, vapor, or gas used for the purpose of disinfecting or of destroying pests

Hepatitis: a disease of the liver, caused by viral infection

Hypostasis: the migration of blood to the lowest parts of a dead body, caused by the effect of gravity

Lands: the uncut parts of a gun barrel, between the rifling grooves

Latent: present and capable of becoming, though not now visible, obvious, or active

Mortician: an undertaker

Pathologist: an alternative description of a medical examiner

Perjure: to voluntarily give false testimony in court

Postmortem: meaning "after death," this is an alternative name for autopsy

Refractive index: a measurement of how much a beam of light is bent on passing through glass or any transparent medium

Rifling: spiral grooves cut along a gun barrel

Rigor mortis: the gradual stiffening of the body's muscles after death

Serology: the laboratory analysis of blood serum, particularly in the detection of blood groups and antibodies

Smoothbore: having a barrel with an unrifled bore

Spectrometer: a laboratory instrument that identifies elements by the wavelength of light they emit when heated to a high temperature

Toxicology: the study and analysis of poisons

CHRONOLOGY

1813:   Mathieu Orfila publishes his first treatise on toxicology.

1834:   James Marsh develops sensitive test for arsenic.

1839:   Orfila successfully demonstrates arsenic in Marie Lafarge poisoning case.

1876:   Cesare Lombroso (Italy) publishes *L'Uomo Delinquente* (*The Criminal Man*); William Herschel in India, and Dr. Henry Faulds in Japan, introduce fingerprinting.

1889:   Alexander Lassagne (France) identifies bullet by rifling.

1892:   Sir Francis Galton publishes *Fingerprints*.

1897:   Edward Henry's fingerprint system adopted by Bengal government.

1900:   Dr. A. Llewellyn Hall publishes *The Missile and the Weapon*.

1900–02: Karl Landsteiner discovers ABO blood groups.

1901:   Henry establishes Fingerprint Branch at London's Scotland Yard; Paul Uhlenhuth discovers precipitin test to distinguish blood of different animals.

1902:   Fingerprints accepted as evidence in British law; Oliver Wendell Holmes accepts ballistic evidence in U.S. court.

1905:   New York State prisons begin fingerprinting, soon followed by St. Louis police and the U.S. Army, Navy, and Marine Corps.

1906:   Mikhail Tsvet (Russia) first develops chromatography.

1911:   Fingerprints as evidence confirmed by Illinois Supreme Court.

1926:   Comparison microscope introduced.

1927:   Harry Battley introduces new cataloging system for fingerprints at Scotland Yard; Landsteiner discovers MN blood groups.

1942:   Palm print accepted as evidence in a British court.

1953:   Francis Crick and James Watson announce structure of DNA.

1968:   Arsenic poisoning of Charles Hall in 1871 proved by neutron activation analysis.

1971:   Glove print accepted as evidence in British court.

1975:   Edward Southern develops "Southern blot."

1983:   DNA fingerprinting developed in Britain by Alex Jeffreys.

1987:   DNA evidence first accepted in Britain.

1994:   Criminal trial of O.J. Simpson fails, due to suspect evidence.

1995:   Aum Shirikyo sect gas attack in Tokyo subway.

2001:   Effective completion of Human Genome Project announced.

FURTHER INFORMATION

Useful Web Sites

www.demon.co.uk/forensic
www.tncrimlaw.com/forensic
forensic.to/forensic.html
www.csfs.ca
www.forensicdna.com
ncfs.ucf.edu
dir.yahoo.com/Science/Forensics
www.ssc.msu.edu/~forensic/link
wwwscience.murdoch.edu.au
www.llnl.gov/str/Forensic.html
www.fsalab.com
www.criminology.fsu.edu/faculty

Further Reading

Campbell, Andrea. *Forensic Science*. Broomall, PA: Chelsea House, 1999.

Evans, Colin. *The Casebook of Forensic Detection*. New York: Wiley & Sons, 1996.

Fisher, Barry A.J. *Techniques of Crime Scene Investigation*. New York: Elsevier, 1992.

Fisher, David. *Hard Evidence*. New York: Simon & Schuster, 1995.

Genge, Ngaire E. *The Forensic Casebook: The Science of Crime Scene Investigation*. New York: Ballantine Books, 2002.

Innes, Brian. *Bodies of Evidence*. Pleasantville, NY: Reader's Digest, 2000.

Quigley, Christine. *The Corpse: A History*. Jefferson, NC: McFarland, 1996.

Saferstein, Richard. *Criminalistics: An Introduction to Forensic Science*. Upper Saddle River, NJ: Prentice Hall, 2001.

Scott, Gini Graham. *Homicide*. Los Angeles: Roxbury Park, 1998.

Wecht, Cyril. *Grave Secrets*. New York: Onyx, 1998.

About the Author

Dr. Brian Innes has been writing on criminal subjects since 1966, when he began work on a series that included *The Book of Pirates, The Book of Spies,* and *The Book of Outlaws.* After contributing to the weekly publication *The Unsolved,* he provided a long series on forensic science, as well as a number of feature articles for *Real Life Crimes*; and his book, *Crooks and Conmen,* was published in 1992.

He has also written *The History of Torture* (1998); *Death and the Afterlife* (1999); and *Bodies of Evidence* (2000), a detailed study of forensic science. He has also contributed commentary for a History Channel feature on punishment. A graduate scientist, Dr. Innes spent a number of years in industry as a research biochemist, and has written extensively on scientific topics, notably for the Marshall-Cavendish *Encyclopedia of Science.* He now lives, and continues his writing, in a converted watermill and former iron forge in southern France.

INDEX